A+ books

3-D Shapes

Pyramids

by Nathan Olson

Capstone
press®

Mankato, Minnesota

A+ Books are published by Capstone Press,
151 Good Counsel Drive, P.O. Box 669, Mankato, Minnesota 56002.
www.capstonepress.com

1 2 3 4 5 6 12 11 10 09 08 07

Library of Congress Cataloging-in-Publication Data
Olson, Nathan.
    Pyramids / by Nathan Olson.
    p. cm.—(A+ books. 3-D shapes)
    Summary: "Simple text and color photographs introduce pyramid shapes and give examples of pyramids in the real world"—Provided by publisher.
    Includes bibliographical references and index.
    ISBN-13: 978-1-4296-0051-4 (hardcover)
    ISBN-10: 1-4296-0051-9 (hardcover)
    1. Pyramid (Geometry)—Juvenile literature. 2. Shapes—Juvenile literature. 3. Geometry, Solid—Juvenile literature.
I. Title. II. Series.
QA491.O46 2008
516'.156—dc22   2006037420

Credits

Jenny Marks, editor; Alison Thiele, designer; Scott Thoms and Charlene Deyle, photo researchers;
    Kelly Garvin, photo stylist

Photo Credits

Capstone Press/Alison Thiele, cover (illustration), 7 (illustration); Karon Dubke, 6, 16–17, 18, 19, 20–21, 22,
    23, 24–25, 26, 29
Corbis/Bill Ross, 13; John Van Hasselt, 15; Mark Bolton, 5; Michael S. Yamashita, 14
Image Farm Inc., 4 (all)
PhotoEdit Inc./Richard Hutchings, 27
Shutterstock/Christophe Testi, 12; Jose Antonio Sanchez, 8–9
SuperStock, Inc./Steve Vidler, 10–11

Note to Parents, Teachers, and Librarians

This 3-D Shapes book uses full color photographs and a nonfiction format to introduce the concept of pyramid shapes. *Pyramids* is designed to be read aloud to a pre-reader or to be read independently by an early reader. Photographs help listeners and early readers understand the text and concepts discussed. The book encourages further learning by including the following sections: Table of Contents, It's a Fact, Hands On, Glossary, Read More, Internet Sites, and Index. Early readers may need assistance using these features.

Capstone Press thanks Troy and Jody Volk for their assistance in making this book.

Table of Contents

What Are 3-D Shapes?

Some shapes have height and width, but no depth. These flat shapes are called two-dimensional, or 2-D shapes.

Other shapes have three dimensions. They are tall, wide, and deep. Pyramids, spheres, and cubes are 3–D shapes.

Pyramids are 3-D shapes that
are biggest at the base and
come to a point on top.

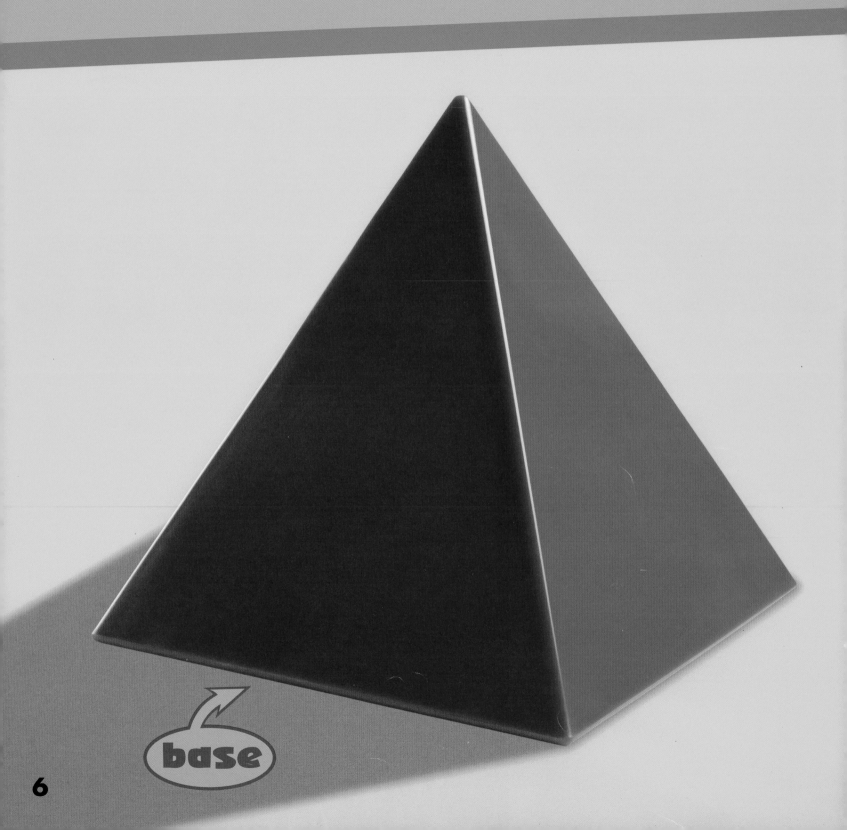

base

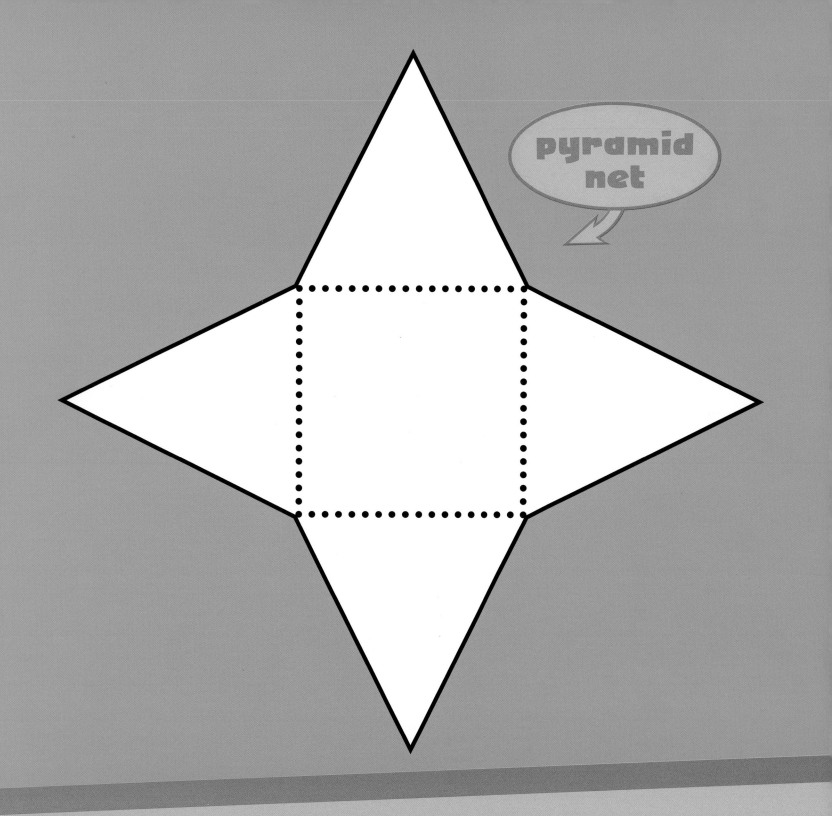

A pyramid is made of four triangles and a square base. These shapes make the pyramid net.

Pyramids around the World

Where can you find pyramids? Let's look for pyramids all around the world.

Some pyramids were built for kings. The Great Pyramid of Giza stands almost as tall as a 50-story building.

This pyramid rises up
in the San Francisco skyline.

Lights make a glass pyramid at the Louvre museum shine brightly at night.

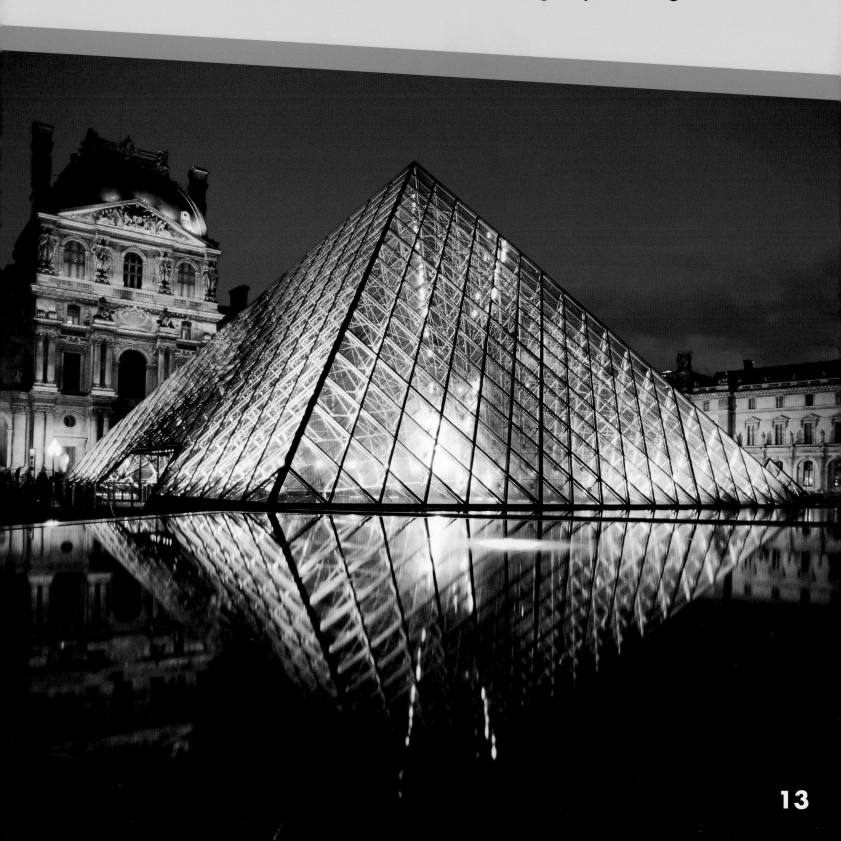

In India, people gather in Hindu temples shaped like pyramids.

Scientists study in this pyramid on Mount
Everest. Glass walls turn sunlight into energy.

Making Pyramids

Why not build your own pyramid? Each layer of blocks is smaller than the one beneath it.

Stacked chocolate candies make
a sweet and melty pyramid.

18

Even wiggly red gelatin can be
molded into a pyramid.

Pyramid Fun

Tying four triangle sides together wraps up a tasty pyramid surprise.

Tiny silver pyramids decorate
a lucky pet's collar.

A colorful pyramid tepee is a great place to play pretend.

Pyramids are cool for swimming around in the pool. Splash!

It's a Fact

 Thousands of years ago, Egyptians buried their kings and queens in pyramids. The room in the center was filled with gold and riches. More than 90 of these royal pyramids still stand in Egypt today.

 Did you know a pyramid is on the back of every $1 bill? This symbol on the dollar means strength.

Most pyramids have a square base and triangle sides. But some pyramids have a triangle base and triangle sides. These 3-D shapes are called tetrahedrons.

 The Pyramid research center on Mount Everest sits 16,568 feet (5,050 meters) above sea level. The building's pyramid shape gives it strength against wind, snow, and rain.

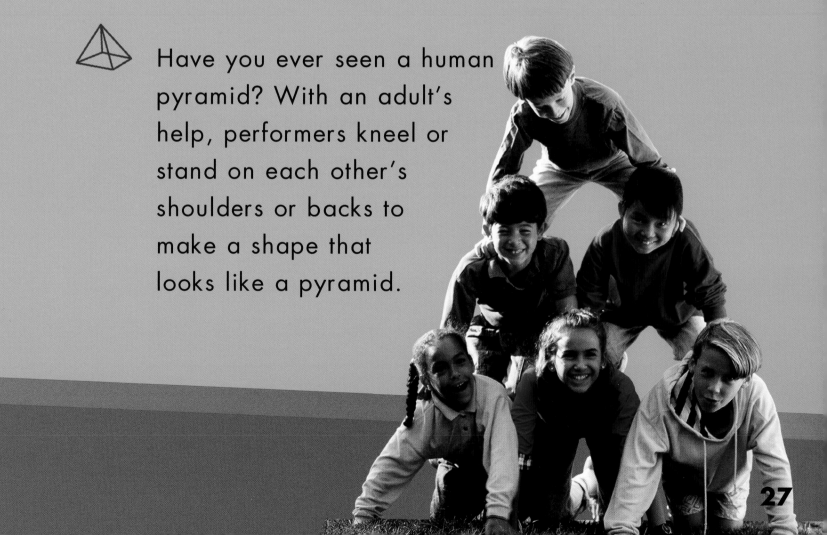 Have you ever seen a human pyramid? With an adult's help, performers kneel or stand on each other's shoulders or backs to make a shape that looks like a pyramid.

Hands On
Perry the Pyramid

You can make a pyramid by folding and taping construction paper into a 3-D shape. Ask an adult to help cut out a pyramid net. Then assemble the pyramid and decorate it to make a funny friend.

What You Need

 pyramid net cut from construction paper

 tape and glue

 scissors

 assorted decorations (felt, buttons, yarn, googly eyes)

What You Do

1 Make folds along the edges of the square (shown in blue dots on the diagram).

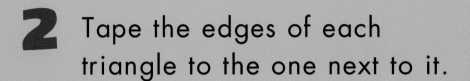

2 Tape the edges of each triangle to the one next to it.

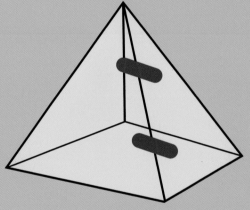

3 Glue decorations on the triangle to make a funny friend called Perry the Pyramid.

Glossary

base (BAYSS)—a flat side that a 3-D shape stands on

cube (KYOOB)—a three-dimensional shape with six square faces

depth (DEPTH)—deepness

sphere (SFIHR)—a round solid shape like a basketball or globe

temple (TEM-puhl)—a building used for worship

three–dimensional (THREE–duh-MEN-shun-uhl)—having length, width, and height; three–dimensional is often shortened to 3-D.

two–dimensional (TOO–duh-MEN-shun-uhl)—having height and width; flat; two–dimensional is often shortened to 2-D.

Read More

Kompelien, Tracy. *3–D Shapes Are Like Green Grapes!* Math Made Fun. Edina, Minn.: Abdo, 2007.

Leech, Bonnie Coulter. *Pyramids.* Exploring Shapes. New York: PowerKids Press, 2007.

Internet Sites

FactHound offers a safe, fun way to find Internet sites related to this book. All of the sites on FactHound have been researched by our staff.

Here's how:

1. Visit *www.facthound.com*
2. Choose your grade level.
3. Type in this book ID **1429600519** for age-appropriate sites. You may also browse subjects by clicking on letters, or by clicking on pictures and words.
4. Click on the **Fetch It** button.

FactHound will fetch the best sites for you!

Index